Track and Field

The marvellous variety of track and
field athletics offers something for
almost every youngster whatever their
strength and stamina. This book,
written and illustrated by ace sports
photographer Tony Duffy, shows the
great international stars, and children
too, in training and in competition.

InterSport

Track and Field

Tony Duffy

Colour photographs by
Tony Duffy
All-Sport Limited

Wayland/Silver Burdett

InterSport

The world of international sport seen through the cameras of some of the world's greatest sports photographers, showing in action both children and the stars they admire.

Basketball	On Horseback
Cycling	Snow Sports
Golf	Soccer
Gymnastics	Swimming and Diving
Ice Sports	Tennis
Motorcycling	Track and Field

Frontispiece: **Split-second Reactions** . . . by both the competitors and the photographer – who has managed to 'freeze' the first surging stride of a 100 m sprint. The start is vitally important in any sprint as a 'fast starter' can steal a couple of metres advantage over his rivals in the first few strides.

First published in 1980 by Wayland Publishers Limited
49 Lansdowne Place, Hove, East Sussex BN3 1HF, England
© Copyright 1980 Wayland Publishers Limited
ISBN 0 85340 777 0

Published in the United States by Silver Burdett Company, Morristown, New Jersey
1980 Printing
ISBN 0–382 06430–5

Phototypeset by Trident Graphics Limited, Reigate, Surrey
Printed in Italy by G. Canale & C.S.p.A., Turin

Contents

What makes an athlete?

Why do some people make better athletes than others? Can you be born with the potential to be a great athlete or is it only through training and coaching that you can become a star in this sport? Both answers are partly true. Some children's bodies are naturally suited to running faster or throwing further than their schoolmates, but almost any healthy young person can become a great athlete if he or she is prepared to work hard by doing the correct training.

So you should not be discouraged if you are not very good at first. Britain's Mary Peters won a gold medal at Munich in the 1972 Olympics when she was 32 years old. She was never very good at athletics either as a child or in her early twenties, but she kept trying. In the end, she beat someone who had always been a fine athlete and who was one of the superstars, Heide Rosendahl of Germany.

There is an athletic event for every type of person. Short, stocky children often make the

On the Road to Victory – Frank Shorter eats up the ground with his long strides on his way to win the Tokyo Olympic Marathon.

7

best sprinters, while thinner ones might find that they are good at long distance running. Large, heavy children have bodies that are just right for the throwing events. If you are not like any of these, you might still find you are good at the decathlon (ten different events) or the pentathlon (five different events).

You can join the junior part of an athletic club in the area where you live. You will develop your athletic skills with the help of good coaching and regular competition. Most of the great stars you will find in the following pages started their careers in clubs. You will need a lot of self-discipline to train. There are no short cuts or easy roads to success, and you have to learn to accept defeat sometimes. But you will find that the more you put into athletics, the more you will get out.

The Launching Pad – Mike Winch of Great Britain about to launch the 7.257 kg (16 lb) shot from the circle. For all his bulging muscles, Mike Winch is 'small' compared to some of the giants who compete in the shot put.

Get Set! . . A field of young girls wait eagerly for the gun to signal the start of a race during the Schools Championships.

Sprinting

The sprints are races over 100 metres and 200 metres, and many people think that 400 metres now qualifies as a sprint race too. The winner of an Olympic sprint can claim the title of the world's fastest man or woman. There is a special thrill in seeing just how fast a human being can run. The fastest speeds ever recorded are 43.5 km/h (27 mph) by American Bob Hayes and 38.6 km/h (24 mph) by the East German woman Marlies Gohr. Of course, when you compare this with the fastest animal, the cheetah, which can run at 96.5 km/h (60 mph), it may not seem so impressive.

World records continue to be beaten as better food, better medical care and scientific advances make people bigger and stronger. But one day, someone will set an ultimate record – one which cannot be beaten. The first ultimate record is likely to be set in the 100 metres, as records for this event have continued to improve over the last thirty years. This is largely due to the synthetic track surfaces now in use, which give more bounce than the old-fashioned grass or cinder

Technical Perfection – Valery Borzov of Russia is one of only a handful of white men who, in recent years, have challenged the dominance of the black athletes in the sprint events.

tracks, and also because of better track shoes. Electronic timing enables the winner's time to be calculated to one hundreth of a second.

Black athletes have always been particularly good at the sprints. Alberto Juan-

Giving Their All – All the strain, effort, and pain that a determined and dedicated athlete has to face is shown through the expressions of these young athletes.

torena, the giant Cuban, was the Olympic champion for 400 metres in 1976. Don Quarrie of Jamaica is a good example of a natural sprinter, one who seems to have been born to be a great athlete. He won the 200 metres in the 1976 Olympics at Montreal and has been

All Eyes On the Finishing Tape – The 100 m sprint is the most explosive Olympic Track Event. A top class sprinter must be able to reach top speed very quickly, and sustain that speed for the whole race. The difference between a winner and a loser can often be as little as a very small fraction of a second.

exceptional in staying at the top for ten years. Normally sprinters do not stay long at the top because the competition is so fierce.

Only two white men have won the Olympic 100 metres since 1932 – they are Armin Hary of Germany and Valery Borzov of Russia. Some people call Borzov a 'manufactured' runner because he has been trained by scientists and coaches who have each taught him one aspect of the sprints – the start, the acceleration and so on. Borzov won both the 100 metres and the 200 metres in the 1972 Olympics.

Although black men have dominated the sprints events, among the women it is the Europeans who have been the most successful. Over the last ten years, the East and West Germans have been at the top of world competition. Two East German girls have been particularly successful. They are Marita Koch who is the current world record holder for 200 metres and 400 metres, and Marlies Gohr, champion of the 100 metres and the fastest lady in the world, though she is being strongly challenged by Evelyn Ashford of America.

Jamaica's Jet – Don Quarrie of Jamaica takes a bend during a 200 m sprint. Quarrie has stayed at the top for longer than any other sprinter in the world. He was the 1976 200 m Olympic champion.

Middle distance

Follow the Leader – A bird's-eye view taken during a 5000 m race. Tactics play an important part in the longer track events. Athletes are often quite happy to 'pad' around the track after the leader for lap after lap in the hope, and belief, that they can 'break' the opposition with a blistering last couple of laps – or even an explosive sprint down the finishing straight (below).

Middle distance races are held at 800 m, 1500 m, 5000 m and 10,000 m. The mile race is no longer run at the Olympics or any other major championship and the 1500 m takes its place.

A runner needs both speed and endurance for middle distance races. The 800 m is now almost a sustained sprint and even in the 10,000 m, competitors start sprinting for the tape as far out as three laps. Most of the great middle distance runners have come from four parts of the world.

Great Britain
Sebastian Coe is currently the best middle distance runner, holding world records for 800 m, 1500 m and the mile. His great rival is Steve Ovett. Ovett does just enough to win and seldom breaks records, but he has won the 1500 m for the last two years. In past decades, there have been a number of world

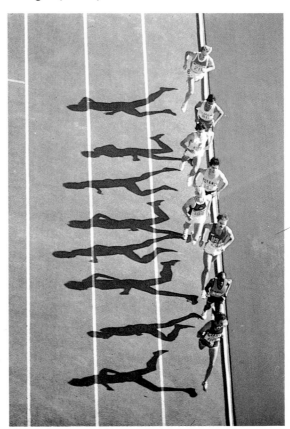

Shoulder to Shoulder – John Walker of New Zealand (nearest the camera) – one of the greatest 1500 m runners over the last decade (left).

class middle distance runners from Great Britain – like Dave Bedford, Derek Ibbotson and Roger Bannister. Bannister was the first man to break four minutes for the mile in 1954. This was regarded as the ultimate achievement then, but now seventeen-year-olds have done it.

There is Only One Winner – No one can expect to become the greatest athlete in the world overnight. The road to the top is bound to be littered with a number of defeats . . . so any aspiring champion must learn to accept defeat gracefully, and use that defeat to spur them to greater efforts the next time they race.

The Work Before the Glory – Henry Rono of Kenya (on the right) and a fellow countryman train over the hilly countryside of their homeland.

East Africa – Kenya and Tanzania
Most of the best African runners come from
the Nandi Hills, the Rift Valley area of
Kenya. Because of the high altitude there is
less oxygen in the air, and runners need to
work their hearts and lungs harder, so they
become tougher. Boys run miles to and from
school and develop into great distance runners. In 1967, Kip Keino was the first
Kenyan Olympic champion and the tradition
has been kept up by Ben Jipcho, Filbert Bayi
(of Tanzania), and Henry Rono. Rono holds
the world record for 5000 m, 10,000 m and
3000 m steeplechase.

Finland
Although Finland is a small country with a
low population, it has produced a number of
hardy athletes. Paavo Nurmi, the 'Flying
Finn', ran with a stop-watch on his wrist and
collected five Olympic golds in the 1920s and
1930s. In the Olympics of 1972 and 1976,
Lasse Viren achieved the 5000/10,000 m
double.

Australia and New Zealand
Four first-class middle distance runners of
the last twenty years have come from this
area. Herb Elliott trained by running up and
down sand dunes in Australia and he never
lost a race at 1500 m or a mile. Peter Snell, a
burly New Zealander, won the 800/1500 m
double in the 1964 Tokyo Olympics. Another

New Zealander, Murray Halberg, had a withered arm which caused him to alter his running pattern, but he still achieved an Olympic gold. And John Walker became an Olympic champion in the 1970s and was the first man to break 3 mins 50 secs for the mile.

The Incredible Coe – Sebastian Coe of Great Britain strains every nerve and sinew in his body to beat the great Filbert Bayi of Tanzania.

Long distance

The most famous long distance race is the marathon. In 450 B.C., the Greek army defeated the Persians at the Battle of Marathon and a soldier called Pheidippides ran back to Athens with the news. He ran a distance of 41.84 kilometres (26 miles), and when he arrived at the Senate building, he gave his news and then collapsed and died of exhaustion. When the modern Olympics re-opened in 1896 in Athens, the long distance race was run over the course that Pheidippides is supposed to have taken. In 1908, at the London Olympics, it was decided that the runners would complete a lap of the stadium in the presence of the king at the end of the race, and thus another 352 metres (385 yards) was added. So the official distance of the marathon became 42.19 kilometres (26 miles 385 yards).

The marathon is a test of courage and stamina. It is extremely popular in America and races like the Boston Marathon and the New York Marathon attract about 10,000 runners, many of whom are women.

Many people think that a woman will

Out on his Own – Joss Naylor is the undisputed 'King of the Fells'. Fell running is similar to cross-country running but is run over much steeper and frequently longer courses.

A Majestic Massed Start – Hopefuls swarm away from under the battlements of Windsor Castle at the start of the Windsor Marathon. A marathon runner may run as many as 160 kilometres (100 miles) a week in training. Ron Hill of Great Britain once ran over 8000 kilometres (5000 miles) in a single year!

probably hold the world record for the marathon in about twenty years' time, because women are considered to have greater stamina and are better equipped than men to deal with the physical demands of this race. The best woman marathoner at present is Greta Waitz of Norway. She is still thirty minutes behind the best male marathoner, but she achieved her record in only her second marathon race.

Cross-country running is good training for the marathon. It is extremely popular during the winter months in Europe. A form of cross-country, called fell running, is carried out in the Lake District of England. It involves running up and down the hills, which is very gruelling training. The greatest fell runner is the legendary sheep farmer, Joss Naylor, who holds most of the fell records. A similar race called the Pike's Peak race takes place in Colorado.

No Time to Stop – A competitor snatches some refreshment during the Windsor Marathon. During a marathon there are refreshment stations sited at about 11 km (7 miles) from the start and then at every 5 km (3 miles).

Steeplechase and hurdles

The steeplechase began in the last century when, after a day's hunting, gentlemen would race back to the local landmark, which was usually the steeple of the local church.

The modern race is run over 3000 metres (nearly two miles) and is for men only. It has a water jump and three other hurdles to clear on each lap. There are 7½ laps in a race. Towards the end of the race, when fatigue sets in, it requires great courage to tackle these solid 91cm (3 ft) high barriers. The water jump excites the crowd most of all. It is almost impossible to clear the obstacle without landing in the water, and most runners today land with one foot in the water. The Kenyans have dominated this race since 1968 and Henry Rono, the great middle distance runner, holds the 3000 m world record.

There are two hurdles races – the 400 m hurdle and the sprint hurdle. The 400 m hurdle is referred to as the 'man-killer' of track events as it is extremely exhausting. Britain has a long tradition in this event –

In Flight – These two Eastern European competitors demonstrate how it *should* be done.

Lord Burghley in 1928 and David Hemmery in 1968 both won the Olympic crowns. The greatest hurdler in the world today is Ed Moses of America. Women only started participating in this race three years ago. Since then two Russian girls, Marina Makeeva and Tatiana Zelenkova, have lowered the world

'Flowing' over the Hurdles – These young athletes are showing how important it is to stay low and 'flow' over the 1.067 m (3 ft 3 in) hurdles during a 110 m race. One of the competitors has kept too low and has hit a hurdle!

record time by five-and-a-half seconds.

The sprint hurdle is at 110 m for men and 100 m for women. It is sometimes referred to as 'rhythm-sprinting' because it requires a very fast sprint speed plus an ability to maintain a rhythm between ten hurdles evenly spaced along the track. The fastest

He Who Reigns Supreme – Ed Moses of the U.S.A. is the unrivalled 'King' of 400 m hurdling. The 400 m hurdles is often described as the 'killer' race as it absolutely drains most competitors.

31

female sprint hurdler in the world today is
Poland's Graziana Rabstyn, who is closely
followed by the Russian and East German
girls. Among the men, a young American,
Reinaldo Nehemiah, was undefeated in 1979
and also set a new world record. His main

The Most Testing Obstacle – The water jump is the fourth jump in each lap of the steeplechase except the first, and must therefore be jumped seven times during a 3000 m race. There are 28 other hurdle jumps during the course of the race.

rivals are Casanas of Cuba and Munkelt of East Germany.

Throwing events

If you see any group of athletes together, you can always tell which are the throwers among the runners and jumpers, because of their huge size and well-developed muscles. A lot of strength is necessary for all four throwing events. Technique is vital too.

You may hear stories about some athletes taking drugs to make them bigger and stronger so that they can throw further. However, these drugs can only slightly improve your length of throw and they create many physical problems. Whatever happens, do not fall into this trap. In any case, drugs are banned and if you are caught taking them, you will be barred because you will be guilty of cheating. Tests are carried out to ensure that no one is taking any drugs.

The four throwing events are shot put, discus, javelin and hammer throwing.

Shot put

The shot is an object shaped like a cannon-ball. The athlete throws from within a circle measuring only 2.13 m (7 ft) across. He or she must not step out of this circle. Eastern

The Awesome Power of the East – East Germany's Ilona Slupianek composes herself before exploding into action.

Europeans and Americans have been at the top of the men's event for many years, and the current world record holder is Udo Beyer of East Germany. Another East German, Ilona Slupianek, has dominated the women's event for some years. It is sometimes regarded as 'unladylike' for women to compete in this event, but at least it does give the large, heavy women a chance to excel in athletics.

Discus
This is a very beautiful event to watch. The discus is shaped like a saucer and you spin around with it in your hand before you release it. The athlete throws from a circle that is 248.9 cm (8 ft 2 in) across. This event is more graceful than the shot put. The thrower needs to move at great speed across the circle while keeping balance. Watch Olympic champion Faina Melnik balance on one foot while she spins across the circle. When the discus is released, it goes spinning through the air rather like a frisbee. This event requires a lot of strength and also the skill to release the discus at the right angle. The current world record holder is Wolfgang Schmidt of East Germany.

Javelin
Early man used spears to kill wild animals or other warriors. Now, in athletics competitions, the javelin thrower runs up to a line

The Great Olympian – Al Oerter of the U.S.A. dominated the discus event for almost two decades! This picture was taken during the Melbourne Olympics of 1956.

A Modern Expert of a Very Ancient Art – Javelin throwing is one of the earliest of all competitive sports. Here Tessa Sanderson of Great Britain is about to launch her javelin high into the air above the stadium (left).

Getting the Point! – The coach explains the 'ins and outs' of the javelin to a group of young athletes.

which can be up to 30 metres (33 yards) away and throws the javelin as far as he can. Strength is not as important as in the other throwing events; mobility, speed, and technique are of greater importance. Throwing the javelin demands the most all-round fitness of all the throwing events. It is also the only event which does not take place in a circle.

In the men's event, the Finns have always led the way, with the Russians and West Germans not far behind. Among the women, Britain has two talented athletes – Tessa Sanderson, the 1978 Commonwealth Games champion, and Fatima Whitbread, the 1979 European junior champion. America's Kathy Schmidt set the world record in 1979.

Hammer throwing

The hammer is a ball weighing 7.25 kg (16 lb) attached to the end of a length of wire which must not be more than 1.22 m (4 ft) long. It is not considered to be a suitable event for women, and only men compete. Once again, the thrower performs within a circle. The men begin by standing in the 2.13 m (7 ft) circle. They suddenly spin round three or four times with the hammer at full arm's length and then release it. These fast turns require exceptional balance and nimbleness – which is always amazing to watch as the men are so large!

It is a dangerous event and the circle is surrounded by a wire cage to prevent the hammer going out on one side and hitting spectators or runners. Karl-Heinz Riehm of West Germany and Yuri Seydich of Russia fight each other for supremacy in this event.

The Russian Hammer – Yuri Seydich of Russia is one of the finest hammer throwers in the world. Great strength and speed 'in the circle' is required in this field event.

The jumps

High jump

The most popular technique among athletes for high jumping used to be the 'straddle' jump. The jumper straddles the bar as he clears it and by the time he reaches the high point of his jump, he is facing downwards. Valery Brumel of Russia became the first man to clear 2.13 m (7 ft) using this technique.

Then came the 'Fosbury Flop', introduced at the 1968 Olympics by the American champion Dick Fosbury. He ran at the bar, jumped up and swivelled over on to his back. This was totally different from the straddle for now the body was facing upwards while clearing the bar. Most of today's top jumpers use this technique although some still prefer the straddle.

Can you imagine being able to jump up to a height that is almost 60 cm (about 2 ft) above your head? Franklin Jacobs of America jumped 59.06 cm (1 ft 11¼ in) above his own height when he cleared 2.32 m (7 ft 7¼ in). And a woman, Tamami Yagi of Japan, cleared 1.90 m (6 ft 2¾ in) although

Up and Over – Rosie Ackerman of East Germany flies elegantly over the high jump bar – which if she was standing directly underneath it would be above her head!

she is only 1.64 m (5 ft 4½ in) tall.

What is the record height reached in the high jump? The current men's world record is 2.34 m (7 ft 8¼ in) and the next barrier we can expect to see broken is the 2.44 m (8 ft) barrier. It is hard to believe that someone could jump that high, but it will probably happen.

Long jump

The farthest anyone has ever jumped is 8.90 m (29 ft 2½ in), which was the incredible length of American Bob Beamon's leap in the 1968 Mexico Olympics. The previous world record was 8.23 m (27 ft) so he beat this by a long way and indeed no one has yet come near his record. The honours are still with America, however, as Larry Myricks is currently the best male jumper in the world. The current women's world record holder is a Russian – Wilma Bardauskiene who was the first woman to clear 7 m (nearly 23 ft), in 1978.

Triple jump

This is called the triple jump because there are three movements – the hop, the step and the jump. Novices do not usually have sufficient triple jump strength and many contestants suffer ankle injuries competing in the triple jump because of the pounding the joints take. The event has recently been dominated by a Russian, Victor Saneyev,

'Leg Shoot' at landing – Sand flies as Karen Murray tries to 'shoot' her legs as far forward as possible on landing – without then toppling over backwards!

'Hanging' in the Air – Speed and precision on the 45 m (147 ft 6 in) long runway are all important to the long jumper. The jumper must be able to 'hit' the 20 cm (8 in) wide wooden take-off board whilst running at full speed (left).

45

who has won the 1968, 1972 and 1976 Olympic triple jump events. Women do not take part, although there is no reason why they should not.

Pole vault
This is possibly the most dramatic of the field events. The vaulters speed down the runway with poles outstretched like knights of old brandishing their lances. The end of the pole is planted in a 'tin' or 'box' at the base of the jump, then the vaulters catapult themselves through the air and over the bar. They are able to fling themselves through the air because the fibreglass poles bend. Whereas long jumpers tend to be tall, vaulters can be small because it is gymnastic ability that is the most important attribute for the vaulter. The vault is the most dangerous of the jumping events and care must be taken over the equipment used and the landing space provided.

The Human Catapult – The pole vault is perhaps the most dramatic and exciting field event for the spectators.

Pentathlon and Decathlon

The pentathlon and decathlon discover the greatest all-round female and male competitors. The winners will have gained the highest overall scores from a series of points awarded for each event. The women have to compete in five events, though there are plans to change the pentathlon into a heptathlon by adding the 200 m and javelin to the current five events, the 100 m hurdles, long jump, high jump, shot put and 800 m. The men compete in ten events: 100 m 400 m, 1500 m, 110 m hurdles, long jump, high jump, shot put, pole vault, discus and javelin.

The events all take place over two days. In the Montreal Olympics of 1976, Bruce Jenner of America won the decathlon, becoming a superstar overnight. But Britain's Daley Thompson is the youngest and most gifted of the current decathletes. Among the women, Diane Jones-Konihowski of Canada and Jane Frederick of America are the names to watch out for.

The Complete Athlete – Daley Thompson of Great Britain is perhaps the most talented all-round male athlete in the world.

Speed and Stamina – Daley Thompson is a world-class sprinter in his own right.

Relay running

There are two relay races, the 4×100 m (400 m relay) and the 4×400 m (1600 m relay). All the other track and field events are for individual competitors and perhaps the relays were introduced to foster team spirit.

In the sprint relay, or 400 m relay, it is very often the team that passes the baton most quickly and efficiently that triumphs over the team with the fastest individual runners. The baton is passed three times, from the first to the second runner, from second to third and third to fourth. In Olympic competition, the passing must take place within a zone or box which is 20 metres (22 yards) long, and failure to pass within this box results in disqualification. In the 1600 m relay, the baton is passed at the completion of each lap. The American team is usually successful in the men's event and the East German girls tend to dominate their event.

Relay races can be enjoyed at school and at clubs where they are often used for warming up.

The Vital Take-Over – No matter how fast the four athletes who make up a sprint relay team are individually – unless they can change the baton smoothly, quickly and safely, they will have little chance of winning.

Organized Chaos! – The first take-over in a 4×100 m relay is often the most hazardous as most of the teams will be attempting to pass the baton at virtually the same time. The baton must be handed over within a take-over zone which is 20 m (22 yards) long.

The superstars

Who are the really great athletes among the men?

Sebastian Coe can claim to be one of the all-time greats, although it is unlikely that he would say so himself since he is the most modest of men off the track. He weighs only 58.5 kg (9 stone 3 lb) and is 1.76 m (5 ft 9¼ in) tall. He is the current world record holder for the 800 m, 1500 m and the mile, the first man to hold all three records at the same time. Perhaps the most surprising thing of all is that these records were all set within such a short space of time – over forty-one days in 1979. Something else that is unusual about Sebastian Coe is that he is trained by his father who has no athletics background.

Sebastian first showed promise when he gained a bronze in the 1500 m in the 1975 European Junior Championships. Since then, he has improved rapidly and uses his speed to great effect.

A very different man from Sebastian Coe, a giant with a huge stride, dominated the middle distance races in the 1976 Olympics.

The Phenomenal Finn – Lasse Viren of Finland astounded the world by retaining both his 5000 m and 10,000 m Olympic titles at the Montreal Olympics in 1976.

This was *Alberto Juantorena* of Cuba, who set a new world record in the 800 m. He is nicknamed 'El Caballo' '(the horse') because of his amazing stride and strength.

Lasse Viren continues in the tradition of strong Finnish athletes and has won both the 5000 m and 10,000 m events in two successive Olympics (Munich, 1972 and Montreal, 1976).

Two athletes stand out among the women. They are Irena Szewinska and Marita Koch.

Irena Szewinska, the tall Polish athlete, is arguably the greatest female athlete of all time. As an inexperienced eighteen-year-old at the 1964 Tokyo Olympics, she captured the silver medal in the long jump and the 200 m. In 1965, she set world records for the 100 m and 200 m. In the 1968 Olympics she won the 200 m in world record time. In the 1972 Olympics, she won two bronze medals, and in 1973 she set world records for the 200 m and 400 m.

Having been successful in events ranging from the long jump to the sprint, she then concentrated her efforts on the 400 m and won the 1976 Olympics in a new world record. No other woman athlete has had sixteen years at the top and Irena will retire after the Moscow Olympics.

In 1979, *Marita Koch*, a twenty-two-year-old from East Germany, beat the legendary Irena Szewinska over 400 m, setting a new world record. She too has smashed the world record at 200 m and has improved on her 400 m record set in 1979. She is currently studying medicine at the University of Rostock and plans to specialize in sports medicine.

The East German Express – Marita Koch of East Germany has taken over the crown of 'greatest female athlete' formerly held by the great Irena Szewinska of Poland.

The road to success

Athletics training in schools forms the grass roots of track and field competition. In America, the high school programme is very competitive and produces many talented young people. In Britain, the A.A.A. 5-Star award scheme gives certificates and badges to children who attain certain standards in each event. The School Championships is a mini Olympics with an opening and closing ceremony and a parade of the teams which come from the various counties. Many schools champions go on to represent their country at the Olympic Games.

However, many children, especially girls, lose interest in athletics when they leave school and their talents are lost to the sport. Hopefully the clubs, with their junior sections, will attract more new members.

In the last decade there has been a European Junior Championship – for the under-nineteen-year-old girls and for the under-eighteen-year-old boys. This has been an extremely successful event and is now held every two years.

For further information about junior athle-

An Olympic Champion in the Making? – Many schools champions go on to represent their country in the Olympic Games. It is, however, essential that young athletes join the junior section of an athletics club so that their talent can be expertly guided after leaving school.

tics, you can write to the *Amateur Athletics Association, 70 Brompton Road, London SW3* if you live in Britain, or to the *Amateur Athletic Union, AAU House, 3400 West 86th Street, Indianapolis, Indiana 47268* if you live in America.

The Open Stage – Young athletes parade during the opening ceremony of the Schools Championships.

Preparing for competition

No athlete, however talented, can produce his best in competition without having the right training behind him. The most important training time is in the winter months when there are no competitions, except for a few indoor meetings which do not include all the athletics events.

Some athletes are fortunate enough to have excellent training facilities close at hand. If you are not so lucky, this need not stop you preparing adequately. It is always possible to make your own training arrangements. For example, some athletes build shot put circles or even long jump pits in their own back gardens. Of course, you should get some expert advice before you do this, so that you do not run any risk of injury through faulty equipment. Those training for the track events are usually luckier than those who want to compete in field events, as there are usually local running tracks. More specialized equipment is needed for the throwing events and for the jumps.

Track and field is like a bank account. You put in the deposit of training and take out

Success Comes to He Who Works – The great Steve Ovett of Great Britain spends many hours training on strength-sapping sand dunes. Sand is one of the most tiring terrains to run over. Success on the track is often directly related to the amount of hard work an athlete puts in during training.

the reward of success in competition. There is no easy way to success and the amount of training you have put in will always show up in the end.

It is also vital to warm up directly before any competition. If you do not warm up by doing various loosening up exercises, your body will be stiff and cold and will not be able to respond to the demands you will be making on it. This is why you see athletes wearing track suits right up to the moment when the competition begins.

As so many track and field events are very technical in nature, it is essential to have a good coach. Your coach is usually also a friend and general adviser on any problems you come up against in your training. It is not uncommon for a parent to be an athlete's coach as they usually know their children better than anyone else. Except in the case of Sebastian Coe, parents who take on this job have usually had athletics training themselves.

The one vital ingredient that an athlete cannot learn is the competitive spirit. You perhaps know some people who hate to lose and these are very often the people who make the best athletes. In many events, the competitors are an even match physically, but it is the person who wants to win the most who usually makes it to the tape first.

Whether you win or lose, it is important that you accept the result in a sportsmanlike

Aiming to Stay at the Top – A world champion like Kathy Schmidt of the U.S.A. trains for hours a day to reach the technical expertise, fitness and strength necessary for her to throw the javelin further than anyone else.

way. Being a modest winner and a gracious loser is the sign of being a true athlete. The Olympic motto says that 'the important thing is not winning but taking part'. Many of today's athletes do not agree with this principle. They feel that the important thing is to win and that is why they are present at the competition. This attitude is healthy provided that they accept defeat graciously if they do not win. Of course, the most thrilling moment of all is when you not only win but set a new world record as well.

Sportsmanship . . . the Vital Ingredient –
Win or lose, the most important thing for any young athlete is to compete and feel part of the 'track and field' family.

Index